FUSS-FREE. GLUTEN-FREE
PLANT-BASED RECIPES

Deliciously VEGAN SOUP Kitchen

SIBEL HODGE

Deliciously Vegan Soup Kitchen
Sibel Hodge
Copyright © Sibel Hodge 2019

The moral right of the author has been asserted. All rights reserved in all media. No part of this book may be reproduced or transmitted in any form by any means, electronic or mechanical (including but not limited to: the Internet, photocopying, recording or by any information storage and retrieval system), without prior permission in writing from the author and/or publisher.

The author acknowledges the trademarked status and trademark owners of various products referenced in this work, which have been used without permission. The publication/use of these trademarks is not authorized, associated with, or sponsored by the trademark owners.

Disclaimer: This book is not intended as health/dietary advice, and it does not replace any medical/health advice given to you by your doctor. All labels and packaging should be checked thoroughly by the reader to ensure they are using a gluten-free/vegan product. The author and publisher disclaim all liability in connection with the use of this book.

Contents

Vegetable Stock 1
African Peanut Soup 2
Bean, Rice, and Spinach Soup 3
Broccoli and Vegan Cheese Soup 4
Butter Bean Soup 5
Carrot and Coriander Soup 6
Chilli Bean Soup 7
Chinese Hot And Sour Soup 8
Chinese Noodle Soup 9
Chunky Minestrone Soup 10
Coconut, Ginger, and Carrot Soup 11
Creamy Corn Soup 12
Daal Curry Soup 13
Festive Chestnut Soup 14
Garden Vegetable Soup 15
Gut-Healing Broth 16
Jackfruit and Courgette (Zucchini) Soup 17
Lentil and Rocket Soup 18
Minted Pea Soup 19
Moroccan Sweet and Sour Soup 20
Mushroom Soup 21
Onion Soup 22
Pistachio Soup 23
Rich Miso Soup 24
Roasted Vegetable Soup 25
Rocket and Vegan Cheese Soup 26
Rustic Leek and Potato Soup 27
Smoky Spanish Chickpea Soup 28
Spicy Pepper and Potato Soup 29
Split Lentil Soup 30
Sweet Potato and Squash Soup 31

Thai Green Curry Soup 32
Tofu and Green Tea Soup 33
Tomato and Carrot Soup 34
Tunisian Spiced Cauliflower and Almond Soup 35
Vegetable and Pasta Soup 36

About the Author 37
Also by Sibel Hodge 38

A big plant power welcome to you…

I'll get the intro bit out of the way quickly so you can get to the good bit…food!

Whether you're a new vegan, or you're dabbling in plant-based foods and want to find exciting, healthier alternatives to your diet, or you already don't use animal products at all, this book is for everyone wanting to explore a vegan diet. The explosion of veganism means an abundance of amazing culinary delights and exciting new plant-based options than ever before. I've been cooking vegan food for four years and the choices have grown exponentially in such a short time. The beauty of this cookbook is that the recipes are quick, fuss-free, easily made gluten-free (gluten-free markers are added in the recipe where needed in brackets), and you won't need any specialist ingredients. There's nothing worse than buying a cookbook, reading through the recipes, and then banging your head against the kitchen worktop because you've discovered you need a particular blend of this, or an obscure jar of that, and you just can't get hold of it. You'll probably find most of the ingredients used in this cookbook already lurking in your store cupboard or, failing that, your local supermarket will stock everything you need.

For those who don't know me, let me tell you a little bit about how this book was born. Usually, you can find me writing novels, but I also have a special love of food and have been cooking since I was about ten years old. Under the watchful eye of my nan, who was a fabulous chef, I developed a love of food that's lasted…let's see…ahem, at least eleven years (yes, I can still be twenty-one in my head), and she taught me how to make mouth-watering meals from scratch. My love of Mediterranean food went on to spark my interest into a vast wealth of international dishes. Increasing your recipe bank means you can travel all over the world, and sample all kinds of cuisine, without ever needing your passport. I'm also a qualified health and fitness professional, with a special interest in nutrition. We all live busy lives these days, don't we? But that doesn't mean we have to swap healthy, easy-to-cook, delicious meals for junky fast food. We are what we eat, and if we put rubbish in, it won't be long before we're feeling rubbish, too. I want to show you that healthy, plant-based, whole-food meals are exciting, taste great, *and* are easily prepared. The recipes included are some of my favourite dishes that I use frequently. Some were originally naturally vegan and some have been adapted since I became vegan. They're all packed with plant power, and I hope you enjoy them as much as me.

Maybe now would be a good time to let you into my little secret (stands up and coughs)… I have a serious soup fetish! There, I confessed. Whatever time of year, you'll find me eating the stuff. I'm a regular soup-a-holic, and I know that I'm not alone in this little culinary foible. I mean, how can you not love a bowl of goodness that's so versatile? Whether you're looking for a simple starter, a light lunch, or a hearty dinner, soup is the perfect comfort dish every time.

These recipes should be used as a guideline because you know your taste buds better than anyone else does. If you want to substitute one veg or spice for another that you like more, then go for it. This is how great recipes are born, and it's all about making the food work for you.

The most important thing in cooking is to have fun with it, so experiment, eat, and enjoy!

Sibel XX

VEGETABLE STOCK

When you're in a hurry, it's super convenient to grab a stock cube out of the cupboard, pour on boiling water, and you're ready to go. All of the following recipes in this book use cubes for speed, but if you fancy making your own as a base to use in any soups or stews, it's super easy.

Tip: Whenever you're steaming veggies, keep the water after use and freeze it for stock. It's full of tasty goodness!

1 large onion - quartered
1 tbsp of paprika
1 tbsp of dried oregano
1 tsp of ground turmeric
1 sprig of fresh thyme or 1 tsp of dried thyme
1 large stick of celery and leaves - cut into quarters
3 cloves of garlic - crushed
1 large leek - cut into quarters
1 large carrot - peeled and cut into quarters
2 bay leaves
A bunch of flat leaf parsley
1 ½ pints (about 4 cups) of boiled water
Salt and pepper to taste
1 tbsp of olive oil for frying

1. Fry the onion and leek until soft. Then add all the other ingredients to the pan, bring to the boil, and simmer for 30 minutes.

2. Strain the liquid through a sieve and you have a yummy stock.

AFRICAN PEANUT SOUP

The first time I tried a variation of this dish, I was hooked, and after tweaking the ingredients to my liking, this recipe is my peanutty gift to you. It's spicy, sweet, and packed full of oomph. Your heat-o-meter is the deciding factor on how spicy you make it, so if you want to crank up the heat with more chilli flakes or fresh chillies, fire away.

Peanuts actually belong to the legume family, like beans and peas, so they're not really a nut. They're a fantastic source of protein and contain the important B-complex group of vitamins like niacin, riboflavin, thiamin, vitamin B6, and folates. Niacin can contribute to brain health and blood flow to the brain and this recipe is so easy it's a no-brainer!

2 large spring onions (scallions) - sliced
2 cloves of garlic - crushed and chopped
2 pints of boiled water (about 5 ½ cups) mixed with a (gluten-free) vegetable stock cube
1 large carrot - grated
1 sweet potato - diced
1 yellow pepper - diced
1 red pepper - diced
250g (about 1 cup) of (gluten-free) crunchy peanut butter
2 large tomatoes - peeled and chopped
2 tbsp of tomato puree
1 ½ inch piece of fresh root ginger - peeled and grated finely
¼ - ½ tsp of chilli flakes or 1 - 2 fresh chillies (or more, depending on heat required)
1 tbsp of paprika
Salt and pepper to taste
Olive oil for frying

Garnish:
Chopped peanuts

1. Fry the onions and peppers until soft.

2. Add the other ingredients, bring to the boil, then simmer for 30 minutes.

3. Blitz in a blender or with a hand blender until smooth. Top with the chopped peanuts and serve.

Serves 4

BEAN, RICE, AND SPINACH SOUP

This might sound like a bland dish but the ingredients make a tasty soup combo, and the oyster mushrooms add a meaty touch. If you don't like spinach, try using rocket (arugula) or kale instead.

Like other leafy green veg, spinach is a nutrient-dense food. It's very versatile and fantastic raw or cooked. Spinach is great for your gastrointestinal health, too, and (if you'll forgive me for talking about colons and food at the same time) it works to protect the cells in the colon from the harmful effects of free radicals. Yay for spinach!

2 spring onions (scallions) - sliced
3 large oyster mushrooms - diced
3 cloves of garlic - crushed and chopped
1 ½ pints of boiled water (about 4 cups) mixed with a (gluten-free) vegetable stock cube
1 green cubanelle pepper (or regular bell pepper) - diced
1 x 400g can of cannellini beans - drained and rinsed
2 large tomatoes - peeled and diced
100g of baby spinach
75g (about ½ cup) of rice (brown/white/wild/basmati)
1 large carrot - grated
1 tbsp of paprika
Salt and pepper to taste
Olive oil for frying

Garnish:
Dollop of vegan, dairy-free yoghurt

1. Fry the onions and pepper until soft. Add the mushrooms and fry until a little browned.

2. Add the rest of the ingredients, bring to the boil, then simmer for 25 minutes.

3. Top with some vegan yoghurt and serve.

Serves 4

BROCCOLI AND VEGAN CHEESE SOUP

Broccoli and cheese go so well together, but when I started cooking vegan food four years ago the choice of plant-based cheese was downright scary! Now, I'm super happy to say, you can get amazing vegan cheese at most supermarkets. And delicious artisan cheeses are also becoming more and more available online. I'm using vegan parmesan for its strong punch, but you can use any of your favourite plant-based cheese. The garnish of nutmeg gives this recipe a really warming zing, perfect for a chilly evening.

Broccoli is a member of the cabbage family and has been called a miracle food. It boasts many health benefits, including: detoxification, anti-inflammatory properties, it can increase eye health, support skin repair, contains anti-cancer nutrients, and it's high in fibre. How can you resist such a nutritious veg?

1 onion - diced
2 cloves of garlic - crushed and chopped
1 stick of celery and leaves - sliced
1 large head of broccoli (including stalk and any leaves) - chopped into chunks
1 leek - sliced
1 large potato - diced
2 pints (about 5 ½ cups) of boiled water mixed with a (gluten-free) vegetable stock cube
1 tsp of dried thyme
1 tbsp of paprika
1 tbsp of chives - chopped
75g (about 2 cups) of vegan parmesan cheese - grated
Salt and pepper to taste
Olive oil for frying

Garnish:
Grated nutmeg

1. Fry the onion and leek until soft.
2. Add the other ingredients, except for the cheese, and bring to the boil. Simmer for 25 minutes.
3. Blitz in a blender or with a hand blender until smooth. Stir in the cheese, then top with grated nutmeg and serve.

Serves 4

BUTTER BEAN SOUP

Handwritten note: Far too flavoured/spicy + a bit runny + bright orange — amount of paprika wrong? Not creamy at all!

This was an old recipe I made in my pre-vegan years that previously had pancetta in it. But the beauty of exploring plant-based foods is veganising old dishes and using new alternatives. I can guarantee that this updated recipe has all the smoky flavour of pancetta but without the meat. It's a smooth and creamy soup that's bursting with iron, fibre, protein, and magnesium.

1 onion – chopped
1 leek – sliced
2 cloves of garlic – crushed and chopped
1 ½ pints (about 4 cups) of boiled water with a (gluten-free) vegetable stock cube
2 x 400g cans of butter beans – drained and rinsed
1 tsp of dried thyme
1 large tomato – peeled and chopped
½ tsp of dried rosemary
1 tbsp of paprika
1 tsp of smoked paprika
¼ – ½ tsp of dried chipotle chilli flakes (or more, depending on taste)
Salt and pepper to taste
Knob of vegan, dairy-free butter/olive oil for frying

Garnish:
1 large spring onion (scallion) – sliced and fried

1. Fry the onion and leek until soft and golden.
2. Add the rest of the ingredients, bring to the boil, then simmer for 25 minutes.
3. Blitz in a blender or with a hand blender until smooth and return to the heat.
4. Fry the garnish of spring onion in a little vegan butter until soft and golden. Pour the soup into bowls and top with the onion.

Serves 4

CARROT AND CORIANDER SOUP

Bursting with flavours, this soup is a firm favourite for any occasion. The orange juice and coriander give it a deliciously sweet, tangy flavour, and the colour will brighten up a dreary winter day.

We've all heard that carrots are good for our eyes, but the high levels of beta-carotene can also act as an antioxidant to cell damage and help to slow down the aging of cells. Beta-carotene is converted into vitamin A in our bodies and that's great for preventing premature wrinkling and dry skin. I'm going to be inventing a new carrot and coriander face cream in the near future. Watch this space!

1 large onion - diced
2 cloves of garlic - crushed and chopped
2 pints (about 5 ½ cups) of boiled water with a (gluten-free) vegetable stock cube
2 large carrots - grated
1 tbsp of ground coriander
1 tsp of ground cumin
Juice of one orange
200g (about 1 cup) of red lentils
3 - 4 tbsp of fresh coriander
Salt and pepper to taste
Olive oil for frying

1. Fry the onion until soft.

2. Add the rest of the ingredients, except for the fresh coriander, and bring to the boil. Simmer for 25 minutes.

3. Add the fresh coriander, then blitz in a blender or with a hand blender until smooth.

4. Pour into bowls and serve.

Serves 4

CHILLI BEAN SOUP

This wholesome dish is delicious and filling. Packed full of flavour, it's a winter warmer that's sure to put a spark into those long, dark nights. I'm using cannellini and red kidney beans here, but if you prefer black-eyed beans, black beans, or the borlotti variety, get them in there! Let's get cracking on the soup…

1 onion – diced
3 cloves of garlic – crushed and chopped
1 large carrot – peeled and grated
1 x 400g can of cannellini beans – drained and rinsed
1 x 400g can of red kidney beans – drained and rinsed
1 x 400g can of chopped tomatoes
2 tbsp of dried oregano
1 tsp of ground cumin
¼ – ½ tsp of chipotle chilli flakes (or more, depending on the heat you like)
1 tbsp of tomato puree
1 tbsp of paprika
1 tbsp of (gluten-free) balsamic vinegar or lemon juice
1 ½ pints (about 4 cups) of boiled water with a (gluten-free) vegetable stock cube
2 – 3 tbsp of flat leaf parsley – chopped
Salt and pepper to taste
Olive oil for frying

Garnish:
Vegan, dairy-free cheese – grated *optional*

1. Fry the onions until soft.

2. Add the rest of the ingredients, except for the parsley, and bring to the boil. Simmer for 25 minutes.

3. Stir in the parsley and pour into bowls. Top with grated vegan cheese and serve.

Serves 4

CHINESE HOT AND SOUR SOUP

This aromatic Asian recipe is warming, nourishing, and super delicious. It's full of earthy-rich, umami flavours with a real kick. It only takes around twenty minutes from start to finish so it's perfect if you're in hurry but still want something light and tasty. Feel free to add some cubed tofu (see Rich Miso Soup for preparation) or (gluten-free) noodles to make this a heartier dish.

1 large spring onion (scallion) - sliced
2 cloves of garlic - crushed and chopped
½ inch piece of fresh root ginger - peeled and chopped finely
2 - 3 oyster mushrooms - diced
1 x 200g can of bamboo shoots - drained and rinsed
100g of fresh bean sprouts
2 tbsp of (gluten-free) soya sauce
1 - 2 tsp of (gluten-free) sriracha sauce or other hot sauce (depending on heat required)
1 tbsp of red wine vinegar
1 ½ pints (about 4 cups) of boiled water with a (gluten-free) vegetable stock cube
Salt and pepper to taste
1 tbsp of sesame oil for frying

1. Fry the spring onion until soft. Add the mushrooms until a little browned.

2. Add the rest of the ingredients, bring to the boil, then simmer for 10 minutes.

3. Pour into bowls and serve.

Serves 4

CHINESE NOODLE SOUP

This is my veganised twist on Chinese chicken noodle soup, using jackfruit instead, which is a fantastic plant-based substitute. When preparing jackfruit, simply drain and rinse, then chop off the centre core and discard that part. The consistency when cooked will end up like a shredded chicken breast. Don't worry if you can't get hold of jackfruit, or don't want to use it. It's equally good without! This authentic broth packs a punch in the taste department and will fool even hardened carnivores.

2 large spring onions (scallions) - sliced
2 cloves of garlic - crushed and chopped
1 ½ inch piece of fresh root ginger - peeled and chopped finely
100g of rice noodles
½ can of 400g young green jackfruit in spring water - cored and sliced
100g (about 1 cup) of frozen sweet corn
100g (about 1 cup) of frozen garden peas
3 large mushrooms (oyster/chestnut/shitake) - sliced
2 tbsp of (gluten-free) soya sauce
2 - 3 leaves of Chinese cabbage or 1 baby bok choy - sliced
¼ tsp of (gluten-free) Chinese five spice powder
2 pints (about 5 ½ cups) of boiled water with a (gluten-free) vegetable stock cube
Salt and pepper to taste
1 tbsp of sesame oil for frying
2 tbsp of fresh coriander (cilantro) - chopped

Garnish:
Coriander (cilantro) - chopped

1. Fry the spring onion until soft. Add the mushrooms until a little browned.

2. Add the rest of the ingredients, bring to the boil, then simmer for 10 minutes.

3. Pour into bowls and serve with chopped coriander.

Serves 4

CHUNKY MINESTRONE SOUP

Minestrone is a thick vegetable soup of Italian origin, often with pasta or rice. An early version of minestrone is included in the ancient cookbook *De Re Coquinaria,* which had some very un-plant-based trimmings, such as cooked brains! There are probably hundreds of ways to cook minestrone soup, and my version is rustic, filling, and definitely brainless.

1 large onion - diced
1 large leek - sliced
3 cloves of garlic - crushed and chopped
1 carrot - grated
1 stick of celery and leaves - sliced
1 ½ pints (about 4 cups) of boiled water with a (gluten-free) vegetable stock cube
2 tbsp of tomato puree
1 x 400g can of chopped tomatoes
1 x 400g can of white beans (cannellini or butter beans) - drained and rinsed
4 - 5 leaves of cabbage (Savoy or white) - sliced
25g (about 1 ½ cups) of baby rocket (arugula) - sliced *optional*
¼ - ½ tsp of chilli flakes *optional*
1 tbsp of paprika
1 tbsp of dried oregano
2 - 3 tbsp of flat leaf parsley - chopped
3 tbsp of (gluten-free) vermicelli or small pasta shapes
Salt and pepper to taste
Olive oil for frying

Garnish:
Vegan cheese - grated *optional*

1. Fry the onion and leeks until soft.
2. Add the rest of the ingredients, except for the parsley and pasta, and bring to the boil.
3. Simmer for 30 minutes, then add the pasta and cook for another ten minutes.
4. Stir in the flat leaf parsley, then pour into bowls and garnish with vegan cheese.

Serves 4

COCONUT, GINGER, AND CARROT SOUP

This is a tropically spiced, scrummy soup that's rich in flavour. You can even serve this wholesome dish cold and it still tastes great. I guarantee once you start eating it, you won't be able to stop. OK, I'll stop gushing about it now and let you see for yourself…

2 red onions - diced
1 leek - sliced
1 red pepper - diced
4 - 5 large carrots - sliced
1 x 400ml can of (gluten-free) coconut milk
1 pint (about 3 cups) of boiled water with a (gluten-free) vegetable stock cube
2 inch piece of fresh root ginger - peeled and chopped
1 tbsp of dried ginger
1 tbsp of ground coriander
Salt and pepper to taste
Olive oil for frying

Garnish
Chilli flakes *optional*

1. Fry the onion, leek, and pepper until soft.
2. Add the rest of the ingredients, bring to the boil, then simmer for 25 minutes.
3. Blitz in a blender or with a hand blender until smooth. Top with the flakes of chilli and serve.

Serves 4

CREAMY CORN SOUP

Although sweet corn often gets a bad rep for being a high carb veg, its resistant starch is a slow-to-digest type of carb that's been shown to help with weight loss and, because it contains a high amount of insoluble fibres, it's great for feeding good gut bacteria. This soup is deliciously creamy, rich, and a perfect soul-warming combo.

1 spring onion (scallion) - sliced
2 cloves of garlic - crushed and chopped
1 leek - sliced
1 medium potato - diced
150g (about 1 ½ cups) of frozen sweet corn
180g (about 2 cups) of cauliflower
½ pint (about 1 ½ cups) of dairy-free milk (soya/oat/almond)
1 ½ pints (about 4 cups) of boiled water with a (gluten-free) vegetable stock cube
2 tbsp of nutritional yeast *optional*
75g (about 2 cups) of vegan cheese - grated
2 - 3 tbsp of flat leaf parsley - chopped
1 tbsp of paprika
1 tsp dried thyme
100g (about ¾ cup) of raw cashew nuts
Salt and pepper to taste
1 tablespoon of olive oil for frying

1. Fry the spring onion and leek until soft.

2. Add the rest of the ingredients, except the milk and cheese, bring to the boil, then simmer for 30 minutes

3. Stir in the milk and cheese until heated through. Then blitz in a blender or with a hand blender until smooth.

4. Pour into bowls and serve.

Serves 4

DAAL CURRY SOUP

Daal is an Indian lentil dish that's full of fragrant flavour. Since I love eating daal with rice, and I also love soup, I thought I'd invent a daal curry soup. Lentils have been consumed for at least 7,000 years, and they're an excellent source of low fat protein.

2 onions – diced
1 green pepper – diced
4 cloves of garlic – crushed and chopped
2 inch piece of fresh root ginger – peeled and chopped finely
1 – 2 fresh chillies or ¼ – ½ tsp of chilli flakes (depending on taste)
4 tbsp of fresh coriander (cilantro) – chopped
200g (about 1 cup) of red lentils
1 x 400ml can of (gluten-free) coconut milk
1 ½ pints (about 4 cups) of boiled water with a (gluten-free) vegetable stock cube
50g of baby spinach or rocket (arugula)
1 tbsp of (gluten-free) curry powder
1 tbsp of (gluten-free) garam masala powder
2 tbsp of tomato puree
Salt and pepper to taste
Olive oil for frying

Garnish:
Fresh coriander (cilantro) – chopped

1. Fry the onion and pepper until soft.

2. Add the other ingredients, except for the fresh coriander, and bring to the boil. Simmer for 30 minutes.

3. Stir in the fresh coriander and blitz in a blender or with a hand blender until smooth. Garnish with a little more coriander and serve.

Serves 4

FESTIVE CHESTNUT SOUP

Chestnuts always remind me of Christmas, and this dish is perfect for a festive starter or main meal any time of year. It's a sweet, fruity, and velvety soup that will have any dinner party guest begging for more.

Unlike most other nuts, chestnuts are relatively low in calories and contain less fat, but they're rich in minerals, vitamins, and phytonutrients. And remember…chestnuts are for life, not just for Christmas!

400g (about 3 cups) of peeled and cooked chestnuts
1 red onion – diced
1 leek – sliced
2 cloves of garlic – crushed and chopped
1 carrot – grated
1 stick of celery and leaves – sliced
1 red apple – peeled, cored, and diced
2 pints (about 5 ½ cups) of boiled water with a (gluten-free) vegetable stock cube
Zest of half an orange – grated
Juice of one orange
½ – 1 tsp of dried sage
2 – 3 tbsp of flat leaf parsley – chopped
Salt and pepper to taste
Olive oil for frying

Garnish:
Orange zest – grated

1. Fry the onion and leek until soft.
2. Add the rest of the ingredients and bring to the boil. Simmer for 25 minutes.
3. Blitz in a blender or with a hand blender until smooth. Top with orange zest and serve.

Serves 4

GARDEN VEGETABLE SOUP

This soup is simple, packed with flavour, and the best part is that you can use up any leftover veggies you have from another meal to give you another delicious dish in no time at all.

1 onion - diced
1 ½ pints (about 4 cups) of boiled water with a (gluten-free) vegetable stock cube
2 cloves of garlic - crushed and chopped
1 leek - sliced
100g (about 1 cup) of frozen green beans
100g (about 1 cup) of frozen garden peas
100g (about 1 cup) of broccoli florets - chopped
90g (about 1 cup) of cauliflower florets - chopped
1 tbsp of dried oregano
1 tbsp of paprika
1 tsp of dried thyme
½ tsp of dried chilli flakes (or more, depending on taste)
1 carrot - grated
2 medium sized potatoes - diced
Salt and pepper to taste
Olive oil for frying

1. Fry the onion and leeks until soft.

2. Add the rest of the ingredients, bring to the boil, then simmer for 25 minutes.

3. Blitz in a blender or with a hand blender until smooth.

4. Pour into bowls and serve.

Serves 4

GUT-HEALING BROTH

This gut-healing broth is my veganised alternative to bone broth. It includes a bunch of wholesome, plant-based ingredients – a comforting bowl full of goodness, with a hefty dose of vitamins, minerals, and nutrients. We've got seaweed, which is a great source of omega 3, plus it's got plenty of iron, calcium, and iodine. Mushrooms, containing lots of amino acids. The ground turmeric gives a powerful anti-inflammatory effect. The parsley is loaded with vitamin C. And the leafy greens add an abundance of vitamins and minerals. But, really, you can add whatever ingredients you like or swap some of my suggestions if they're not to your taste. When using the veggie skins, make sure you wash them beforehand.

3 dried shitake mushrooms (dried contains more vitamin D) - roughly sliced
1 inch piece of root ginger with skin - roughly sliced
2 cloves of garlic - peeled and smashed
3 large oyster mushrooms (or any other type) - roughly sliced
1 large carrot with skin - roughly chopped
1 leek - cut into four pieces and halved
100g (about 1 cup) of red cabbage - roughly sliced
1 celery stick and leaves - roughly chopped
Skin peelings of 1 courgette
1 medium sized potato with skin - roughly chopped
1 red onion with skin - quartered
1 chilli pepper - roughly chopped
200g (about 2 cups) of greens (spinach/kale/Savoy cabbage) - roughly sliced
2 tbsp of dried wakame seaweed flakes *optional*

2 tbsp ground turmeric
2 pints (about 5 ½ cups) of filtered water
A bunch of fresh flat leaf parsley
1 tsp of peppercorns
½ tsp of pink Himalayan salt
2 tbsp of nutritional yeast
2 bay leaves
1 tbsp of virgin coconut oil

1. Add everything to the pan, bring to the boil, then simmer for 25 minutes.

2. Strain and serve. You can also freeze any excess.

Serves 4

JACKFRUIT AND COURGETTE (ZUCCHINI) SOUP

The inhabitants of South America have been eating courgettes for several thousands of years, but the courgette we're probably most familiar with these days is a summer squash developed in Italy. It's low in calories and high in vitamin A, vitamin K, and fibre, and added to this recipe, you'll have a wholesome taste of the Med that's great for any time of the year.

This soup uses jackfruit instead of meat, which is a fantastic plant-based substitute. When preparing jackfruit, simply drain and rinse, then chop off the centre core and discard that part. The consistency when cooked will end up like a shredded chicken breast.

1 onion - diced
2 cloves of garlic - crushed and chopped
1 stick of celery and leaves - sliced
½ can of 400g young green jackfruit in water - cored and sliced
1 pint (about 3 cups) of boiled water with a (gluten-free) vegetable stock cube
1 carrot - grated
2 small courgettes (zucchini) - coarsely grated
½ pint (about 1 ½ cups) of dairy-free milk (soya/oat/almond/rice)
100g (about 1 cup) of (gluten-free) penne pasta
2 tbsp of nutritional yeast
1 tsp of dried thyme
1 tbsp of dried mint
Salt and pepper to taste
Olive oil for frying

1. Fry the onion until soft.
2. Add the other ingredients, except for the pasta and milk, and bring to the boil. Simmer for 25 minutes.
3. Add the pasta and cook until soft (approx 10 minutes).
4. Stir in the milk and allow to heat through.
5. Pour into bowls and serve.

Serves 4

LENTIL AND ROCKET SOUP

This soup is a filling, tasty, and nutritious variation of the classic Turkish lentil soup, which is usually served with wedges of lemon to drizzle on top. You can use more or less dried mint if you prefer, but since I'm a minty kind of girl, I always add more. I love the peppery twist that the chopped rocket (arugula) adds to this recipe.

200g (about 1 cup) of red lentils
1 onion- chopped
1 carrot - chopped
1 medium sized potato - chopped
2 cloves of garlic - crushed and chopped
1 ½ tbsp of dried mint
1 tsp of dried thyme
1 tsp of ground turmeric
1 tbsp of paprika
2 - 3 tbsp of tomato puree
25g (about 1 ½ cups) of chopped rocket (arugula)
1 ½ pints (about 4 cups) of boiled water with a (gluten-free) vegetable stock cube
Salt and pepper to taste
Olive oil for frying

On the side:
Lemon wedges

1. Fry the onicn until soft.

2. Add the rest of the ingredients, bring to the boil, then simmer for 25 minutes. As the lentils soak up the liquid you may need to add more stock.

3. Blitz in a blender or with a hand blender until smooth and spoon into bowls.

4. Squeeze fresh lemon juice over the top and serve.

Serves 4

MINTED PEA SOUP

This is a fantastic summer soup. Sweet garden peas, minty freshness, and speedy cooking times make this recipe a keeper. The colour of this soup is gorgeous, and you can tell just by looking at it that it's packed full of earthy goodness. If you want to turn this into a richer soup, then add a touch of vegan, dairy-free cream at the end.

3 spring onions (scallions) - sliced
3 cloves of garlic - crushed and chopped
1 large leek - sliced
500g (about 5 cups) of frozen garden peas
1 ½ tbsp of dried mint
¼ tsp of ground cinnamon
1 ½ pints (about 4 cups) of boiled water with a (gluten-free) vegetable stock cube
Salt and pepper to taste
Knob of vegan, dairy-free butter/olive oil for frying

Garnish:
Chives - chopped

1. Fry the onions and leek until soft.

2. Add the other ingredients, bring to the boil, then simmer for 25 minutes.

3. Blitz in a blender or with a hand blender until smooth.

4. Top with the chopped chives and serve. If you want to add dairy-free yoghurt or cream, go for it!

Serves 4

MOROCCAN SWEET AND SOUR SOUP

This recipe is sweet, spicy, sour, and fun! Moroccan food is all about flavour and colour, and this dish is an explosion of both.

I'm using dried apricots here, and whenever possible try and get apricots that are naturally air-dried, rather than those dried using sulphur or sulphur dioxide, which can cause allergies in some people. The chickpeas provide a great source of dietary fibre, plus they're rich in folate, calcium, and manganese, and also low in fat, which is always a bonus! But if you don't like chickpeas, substitute them for a can of your favourite beans.

1 onion - diced
1 carrot - diced
1 red pepper - diced
1 green pepper - diced
8 - 10 dried apricots - chopped
3 cloves of garlic - crushed and chopped
2 inch piece of fresh root ginger - peeled and chopped finely
1 x 400g can of chopped tomatoes
1 x 400g can of chickpeas - drained and rinsed
Juice of half a lemon
2 - 3 tbsp of chopped fresh coriander (cilantro)
1 pint (about 3 cups) of boiled water with a (gluten-free) vegetable stock cube
¼ tsp of ground cinnamon
1 tbsp of ground coriander
1 tsp of ground cumin
¼ tsp of ground nutmeg
1 tbsp of ground turmeric
1 tbsp of paprika
¼ - ½ tsp dried chilli flakes (or more, if you want it hotter)

¼ tsp of black pepper
Salt to taste
Olive oil for frying

1. Fry the onions and peppers until soft.

2. Add the other ingredients, except for the fresh coriander, and bring to the boil. Simmer for 30 minutes.

3. Stir in the fresh coriander and serve.

Serves 4

MUSHROOM SOUP

For this earthy, comforting soup you can use the everyday kind of mushrooms, like chestnut or button, or you can mix them with more exotic and punchier varieties like oyster, porcini, chanterelles, shiitake, and portobello. Experimenting with different mushrooms will add a whole new dimension to this soup, so have fun with it!

1 large onion - diced
2 cloves of garlic - crushed and chopped
2 pints (about 5 ½ cups) of boiled water with a (gluten-free) vegetable stock cube
1 tsp of dried thyme
½ tbsp of dried oregano
500g (about 6 cups) of mushrooms - sliced
2 tbsp of tomato puree
75g (about ½ cup) of rice (white/brown/basmati/wild)
1 stick of celery and leaves - sliced
Salt and pepper to taste
Olive oil for frying

1. Fry the onion until soft, then add the mushrooms and fry for a couple of minutes.

2. Add the rest of the ingredients, bring to the boil, then simmer for 30 minutes.

3. Blitz in a blender or with a hand blender until smooth.

4. Pour into bowls and serve.

Serves 4

ONION SOUP

This was one of the first soups I was ever taught to make when I was about ten, and I loved it as much then as I do now, although I've tweaked the recipe a little. I think the trick to making fab onion soup is that you need to have a little patience when cooking the onions at the beginning, because it's this process that will make it a lot more flavoursome. The slower they cook, the sweeter and tastier they'll be as they caramelise. If you're having a boozy moment, you can also add a splash of vegan white or red wine.

As well as packing your food with lashings of taste, onions also have many health benefits. They've been used for centuries to reduce inflammation and heal infections, they contain chromium to help regulate blood sugar, and they can help your immune system. Bring on the onions!

3 large onions – sliced
Goggles for slicing onions!
1 leek – sliced
2 cloves of garlic – crushed and chopped
2 pints (about 5 ½ cups) of boiled water with a (gluten-free) vegetable stock cube
1 tsp of dried thyme
1 tbsp of dried oregano
2 tbsp of tomato puree
Salt and pepper to taste
Olive oil or vegan, dairy-free butter for frying

Garnish:
(Gluten-free) bread – toasted
Vegan, dairy-free cheese – grated

1. Fry the onions on a medium heat, stirring continuously until they turn golden brown (they will release some moisture when cooking). Turn the heat up high and carry on stirring as the onions caramelize and go a darker brown. If you don't keep stirring, they'll just stick to the pan and burn, so don't leave them.

2. Add the rest of the ingredients, except for the goggles. Bring to the boil and simmer for 30 minutes.

3. Meanwhile, toast the (gluten-free) bread. Place the bread in bowls and top with grated vegan cheese. Pour the soup over the top and serve.

Serves 4

PISTACHIO SOUP

This soup originates from the Middle East, where it's common to use ground or pureed nuts in cooking. It's a creamy, silky, and nutty dish all rolled into one that will impress anyone. It screams of elegance and sophistication, and I'm sure once you try it, you'll be coming back for more.

Pistachios not only taste great as a snack in their own right, but they're also laden with antioxidants. They can help to lower bad cholesterol and improve eye health and your nervous system. I'm giving them three cheers!

2 large leeks - sliced
2 pints (about 5 ½ cups) of boiled water with a (gluten-free) vegetable stock cube
100g (about 1 cup) of ground, unsalted pistachios
50g (about ¾ cup) of chopped, unsalted pistachios
Juice of 1 orange
Juice of half a lemon
100g (about 1 cup) of ground almonds
1 tsp of ground coriander
1 tsp of ground turmeric
½ tsp of ground ginger
½ tsp of ground cinnamon
1 tbsp of paprika
Salt and pepper to taste
Olive oil for frying

Garnish:
Pistachios and almonds - chopped and toasted

1. Fry the leeks until soft.
2. Add the other ingredients, bring to the boil, then simmer for 20 minutes.
3. Top with the toasted pistachios and almonds and serve.

Serves 4

RICH MISO SOUP

This is a delicious Asian broth, rich in umami flavour, and it's my new go-to hangover cure! It's super quick, taking about ten minutes to prepare and ten more to cook – perfect if you're in hurry. I like to use meaty mushrooms, like oyster or shiitake, but regular chestnut or button mushrooms work just as well.

You don't need to faff around pressing the tofu to get rid of the excess liquid because it's going in a soup. Simply drain the tofu from the liquid it comes in, pat it in some paper kitchen towel, and you're good to go. Miso paste is made from fermented soya beans to give it a rich taste, but not all types are gluten-free so check the paste carefully if you're following a GF diet. I'm using a white miso paste in this dish.

1 spring onion (scallion) - chopped finely
1 inch piece of root ginger - peeled and grated
2 cloves of garlic - crushed and chopped
3 large oyster mushrooms - diced
3 leaves of Chinese cabbage or 2 baby bok choy - sliced
1 large carrot - grated
1 tbsp of (gluten-free) soya sauce
½ block of 350g silken tofu - cubed
2 tbsp of (gluten-free) miso paste
50g (about ½ cup) of frozen peas
2 pints (about 5 ½ cups) of boiled water with a (gluten-free) vegetable stock cube
1 tbsp of dried seafood flakes (wakame/nori) *optional*
Salt and pepper to taste
1 tbsp of sesame oil for frying

Garnish:
A few drops of (gluten-free) soya sauce

1. Fry the spring onions until soft. Add the mushrooms and garlic and fry gently for a few minutes.

2. Add all the other ingredients, except the miso paste, then simmer for ten minutes.

3. Put the miso paste in a jug. Take a ladle full of the soup liquid and add to the paste, stirring until it's dissolved. Then take the soup off the hob, pour in the miso paste liquid, and stir until mixed.

4. Serve with a sprinkling of (gluten free) soya sauce.

ROASTED VEGETABLE SOUP

Roasting veggies is a sure way to add a bit of sparkle in your diet, and I love the way the maple syrup, balsamic vinegar, and oil caramelises the veggies and makes them fabulously sweet. You can use any vegetables you want for this recipe. The only key ingredient is when roasting them, make sure the oven is really hot when you start, and turn them frequently throughout, so they're evenly coated in the juices and the heat is distributed to all of them. This soup has intense flavour and is full of veggie goodness.

2 large red onions – roughly chopped
8 cloves of garlic – in their skins
1 green pepper – roughly chopped
1 red pepper – roughly chopped
1 yellow pepper – roughly chopped
1 aubergine (eggplant) – roughly chopped
1 courgette (zucchini) – roughly chopped
4 large mushrooms – quartered
2 tbsp of maple syrup
2 – 3 tbsp of olive oil
2 tbsp of (gluten-free) balsamic vinegar
2 tsp of dried thyme
1 x 400g can of tomatoes
1 ½ pints (about 4 cups) of boiled water with a (gluten-free) vegetable stock cube
Salt and ground black pepper to taste

Garnish:
Flat leaf parsley – chopped

1. Chop all the veggies into about 2 cm chunks so they're evenly sized, then add them to a large baking tin.

2. In a separate bowl mix the olive oil, maple syrup, vinegar, dried thyme, salt and pepper. Pour over the veggies and toss so everything is covered well.

3. Cook in a preheated oven at 200C/400F/Gas Mark 6 for around 35 minutes until vegetables are soft. Turning every now and then helps them to cook better.

4. Remove the veggies from the oven and put them in a saucepan, remembering to remove the garlic from its skin. Add the tinned tomatoes and stock and bring to a simmer for ten minutes.

5. Blitz in a blender or with a hand blender until smooth, then sprinkle with parsley and serve.

Serves 4

ROCKET AND VEGAN CHEESE SOUP

This soup has a lot of flavours going on. Every mouthful will give you the peppery richness of rocket (arugula) and creaminess from the vegan cheese.

1 large onion – diced
3 cloves of garlic – crushed and chopped
1 large potato – diced
75g (about 2 cups) of vegan, dairy-free cheese – grated
100g of rocket (arugula)
1½ pints (about 4 cups) of boiled water with a (gluten-free) vegetable stock cube
1 tsp of ground coriander
¼ tsp of ground cinnamon
¼ tsp of dried chilli flakes
2 – 3 tbsp of flat leaf parsley – chopped
Salt and pepper to taste
Olive oil for frying

Garnish:
Vegan cheese – grated
Walnuts – chopped

1. Fry the onion until soft.

2. Add the rest of the ingredients, except the cheese, and bring to the boil. Simmer for 25 minutes.

3. Stir in the cheese. Blitz in a blender or with a hand blender until smooth. Pour into bowls and top with a little more vegan cheese and walnuts.

Serves 4

RUSTIC LEEK AND POTATO SOUP

Leek and Potato is such a classic soup, and this variation is chunky, tasty, and yet so simple. Feel free to add a dollop of dairy-free yoghurt at the end as a garnish.

Potatoes get a bad rap sometimes, and are often the first thing people cut out if they want to lose weight, but a boiled new potato only has around 25 calories in it. Keeping the skins on when cooking will increase their fibre and flavanoids to give you extra nutritional content. And don't forget, they're also packed full of goodness, can help to lower blood pressure, and are rich in Vitamin B6

1 large onion - diced
2 large leeks - sliced
2 cloves of garlic - crushed and chopped
1 carrot - diced
2 mediums potatoes - diced
2 sticks of celery and leaves - sliced
2 pints (about 5 ½ cups) of boiled water with a (gluten-free) vegetable stock cube
1 tbsp of paprika
1 tsp of dried thyme
2 - 3 tbsp of fresh flat leaf parsley
Salt and pepper to taste
Olive oil for frying

Garnish:
Flat leaf parsley – chopped

1. Fry the onion and leeks until soft.

2. Add the rest of the ingredients, except for the parsley, and bring to the boil. Simmer for 30 minutes.

3. Stir in the flat leaf parsley, then pour into bowls and serve. Add more parsley as a garnish.

Serves 4

SMOKY SPANISH CHICKPEA SOUP

This little taste of Spain is big on flavour. The smoky hit and the creamy chickpeas give it a full-on taste that makes it scrumptiously special. It's a robust meal in a bowl, great for any time of year. If you don't want to use rocket (arugula), swap it for baby spinach or kale. And if you don't like chickpeas, use cannellini or butter beans instead.

1 x 400g can of chickpeas - drained and rinsed
2 spring onions (scallions) - sliced
2 cloves of garlic - crushed and chopped
1 ½ pints (about 4 cups) of boiled water with a (gluten-free) vegetable stock cube
1 large carrot - grated
3 - 4 mushrooms - diced
1 green cubanelle pepper (or regular bell pepper) - diced
25g (about 1 ½ cups) of rocket (arugula) - chopped
3 tbsp of red lentils
2 large tomatoes - peeled and diced
¼ - ½ tsp of chipotle chilli flakes (or more, depending on taste)
1 tbsp of paprika
1 tsp of smoked paprika
2 tbsp of black olives - deseeded and chopped *optional*
Salt and pepper to taste
Olive oil for frying

1. Fry the onions and peppers until soft. Add the mushrooms and fry for a couple of minutes.

2. Add the other ingredients, bring to the boil, then simmer for 25 minutes.

Serves 4

SPICY PEPPER AND POTATO SOUP

This dish makes a hearty lunch or dinner that's sure to keep the chills away. I've added a little firm tofu for an extra protein hit, but it will still be equally as gorgeous if you want to omit it (see Rich Miso Soup recipe for tofu preparation). If you have time, and you want to make the flavours more intense, you could roast the peppers and onions first (see Roasted Vegetable Soup).

1 x 350g block of firm tofu – cubed
1 large red pepper – diced
1 large green pepper – diced
1 onion – diced
2 medium sized potatoes – diced
1 ½ pints (about 4 cups) of boiled water with a (gluten-free) vegetable stock cube
2 tsp of mustard seeds
1 – 2 tsp of (gluten-free) sriracha sauce (or other hot sauce) or 1 – 2 fresh chillies – diced (depending on heat required)
¼ tsp of ground black pepper
1 tbsp of paprika
2 tbsp of tomato puree
Salt to taste
Olive oil for frying

Garnish:
Flat leaf parsley – chopped

1. Fry the onions and peppers until soft.
2. Add the mustard seeds and stir around for 5 – 10 seconds.
3. Add the other ingredients, bring to the boil, then simmer for 25 minutes.
4. Sprinkle with flat leaf parsley and serve.

Serves 4

SPLIT LENTIL SOUP

This hearty and satisfying dish was inspired by a Greek dip that's made with yellow split peas. High in fibre and protein, this recipe has a wonderful spiciness with a creamy depth to it.

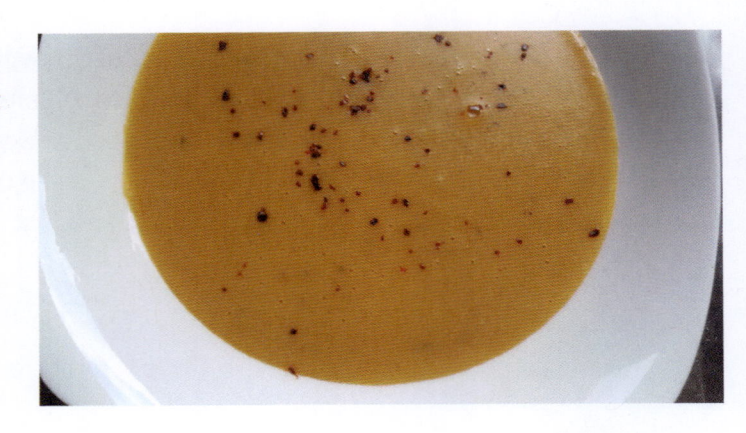

1 onion - diced
1 leek - sliced
2 cloves of garlic - crushed and chopped
250g (about 1 ¼ cups) of yellow split lentils
1 ½ pints of boiled water (about 4 cups) mixed with a (gluten-free) vegetable stock cube
1 medium sized potato - cubed
1 large carrot - diced
1 tbsp of paprika
1 tsp dried thyme
½ - 1 tsp chipotle chilli flakes (or more, depending on taste)
1 tbsp (vegan/gluten-free) Worcestershire sauce
½ pint (about 1 ½ cups) of dairy-free milk (soya/oat/rice/almond)
Salt and pepper to taste
Olive oil for frying

Garnish:
Chilli flakes/sprinkling of cayenne pepper/drizzle of chilli oil

1. Fry the onions and leek until soft.
2. Add the rest of the ingredients, except the milk, and bring to the boil. Simmer for 30 minutes. If the lentils soak up too much liquid when cooking, add a little more stock
3. Blitz in a blender or with a hand blender until smooth.
4. Add the dairy-free milk and stir on the hob to heat through before serving.

Serves 4

SWEET POTATO AND SQUASH SOUP

Sweet potato and squash gives this soup a wonderfully sweet and nutty taste. If you want to intensify the flavour, and you have the time, roast the squash in the oven with a little olive oil. This dish is high in Vitamin A and beta-carotene.

1 ½ pints (about 4 cups) of boiled water with a (gluten-free) vegetable stock cube
1 x 400ml can of (gluten-free) coconut milk
1 large sweet potato - diced
1 small butternut squash - diced
1 red pepper - diced
1 red onion - diced
2 cloves of garlic - crushed and chopped
1 tsp of ground cumin
1 tsp of ground coriander
1 tbsp of paprika
3 tbsp of fresh coriander - chopped
Salt to taste
Olive oil for frying

Garnish:
Fresh coriander - chopped

1. Fry the onion and pepper in a large saucepan until soft.

2. Add the rest of the ingredients, bring to the boil, then simmer for 30 minutes

3. Blitz in a blender or with a hand blender until smooth and garnish with fresh coriander.

Serves 4

THAI GREEN CURRY SOUP

Thai food is an amalgamation of flavours – savoury and sweet, salty and sour, spicy and fragrant, so is it any wonder that it's so popular? This recipe is high on the aromatic taste test but so simple. It's a seductive little Thai fix for any day of the week.

1 x 400ml can of (gluten-free) coconut milk
1 pint (about 3 cups) of boiled water with a (gluten-free) vegetable stock cube
1 – 2 chillies – chopped
2 inch piece of fresh root ginger – peeled and chopped finely
Zest of 1 lime – grated finely
2 tbsp of (gluten-free) soya sauce
2 cloves of garlic – crushed and chopped
2 spring onions (scallions) – sliced finely
4 – 6 oyster mushrooms (or any kind) – sliced
1 green pepper – diced
75g of rice noodles
4 tbsp of fresh coriander (cilantro) – chopped
1 tbsp of sesame oil for frying
Salt and pepper to taste

Garnish:
Coriander (cilantro) – chopped

1. Fry the spring onions and peppers until soft.
2. Add the mushrooms and fry for a couple of minutes.
3. Add the rest of the ingredients, bring to the boil, then simmer for 15 minutes.
4. Top with chopped coriander and serve.

Serves 4

TOFU AND GREEN TEA SOUP

I've been drinking green tea for years and I love the stuff. Lately, I've noticed that it's being used more and more in cooking, from cookies to cakes to main dishes. As weird as it sounds, green tea and tofu goes amazingly well together, so I invented this Asian-style soup. You're getting all the benefits of antioxidants and cancer-fighting properties from the green tea, and the tofu provides a bunch of essential amino acids and a great source of iron and protein. More power to the tofu!

1 x 350g block of firm tofu - diced (see Rich Miso Soup recipe for tofu preparation)
1 red pepper - diced
2 spring onions (scallions) - sliced
2 tbsp of tomato puree
4 large oyster mushrooms (or any kind) - diced
¼ tsp of chilli flakes
1 tbsp of maple syrup
2 tbsp of (gluten-free) soya sauce
1 green tea bag
100g of rice noodles
1 can of baby corn - drained and sliced into bite-size chunks
2 inch piece of fresh root ginger - peeled and chopped
3 cloves of garlic - crushed and chopped
1 ½ pints (about 4 cups) of boiled water with a (gluten-free) vegetable stock cube
1 tbsp of sesame oil for frying
Salt and pepper to taste

Garnish:
Coriander (cilantro) - chopped

1. Fry the onion and pepper until soft. Add the mushrooms a fry for a few minutes.

2. Add the stock, then split open the tea bag and pour the tea flakes into the pan. Add the other ingredients and bring to the boil. Simmer for 15 minutes.

3. Pour into bowls and top with coriander.

Serves 4

TOMATO AND CARROT SOUP

I remember getting the recipe for tomato soup that this dish is based on in my home economics class at school when I was eleven. I fell in love with it because it was so simple but so delicious. In the time since then (ten years, of course!), I've adapted it to the recipe below, and I've cooked it hundreds of times without getting bored of it. It's one of those faithful recipes that you can pull out of your hat for a quick lunch or light dinner. I think this works so well as a rustic, chunky soup but you can also blend it for a smoother dish.

1 ½ pints (about 4 cups) of boiled water with a (gluten-free) vegetable stock cube
1 x 400g can of chopped tomatoes
1 red onion - chopped
1 carrot - grated
2 tbsp of tomato puree
1 tbsp of dried oregano
3 tbsp of (gluten-free) vermicelli or small pasta shapes
Salt and pepper to taste
Olive oil for frying

1. Fry the onion until soft and golden. Add the rest of the ingredients, bring to the boil, then simmer for 20 minutes.

2. Add the pasta and cook for ten minutes before serving.

Serves 4

TUNISIAN SPICED CAULIFLOWER AND ALMOND SOUP

Cauliflower often gets a raw deal. It brings back memories to me of soggy and tasteless school dinners, but it doesn't have to be like that. This recipe will have even the worst cauliflower-haters eating out of your soup bowl.

1 large leek – sliced
1 large stick of celery and leaves – sliced
1 large head of cauliflower – cut into small florets
100g (about 1 cup) of flaked almonds – toasted
½ tsp of ground ginger
½ tsp of ground cinnamon
1 tbsp of ground coriander
½ tsp of ground cumin
¼ tsp of ground nutmeg
1 tbsp of ground turmeric
1 tbsp of paprika
½ tsp of chilli flakes (or more, depending on taste)
2 pints (about 5 ½ cups) of boiled water with a (gluten-free) vegetable stock cube
Salt and pepper to taste
Olive oil for frying

Garnish:
Flaked almonds – toasted
Sprinkling of cayenne pepper/paprika

1. Fry the leek until soft.

2. Add the other ingredients and bring to the boil. Simmer for 25 minutes.

3. Blitz in a blender or with a hand blender until smooth. Top with a sprinkling of cayenne pepper and toasted almonds.

Serves 4

VEGETABLE AND PASTA SOUP

This recipe is so versatile because you can really use any vegetables that you like, or make it a heartier dish by adding some kidney or white beans.

1 x 400g can of chopped tomatoes
1 onion – diced
2 cloves of garlic – crushed and chopped
3 tbsp of flat leaf parsley – chopped
1 ½ pints (about 4 cups) of boiled water with a (gluten-free) vegetable stock cube
1 aubergine (eggplant) – diced
2 medium sized carrots – grated
1 red pepper – diced
1 green pepper – diced
50g (about 1 cup) of (gluten-free) vermicelli or other small pasta shapes
Salt and pepper to taste
Olive oil for frying

Garnish:
Grated vegan cheese *optional*
Flat leaf parsley – chopped

1. Fry the onion, peppers, and aubergine until soft.

2. Add the rest of the ingredients, bring to the boil, then simmer for 25 minutes.

3. Add the pasta and cook for ten minutes.

4. Pour into bowls and garnish.

Serves 4

About the Author

Sibel Hodge is the author of the No 1 fiction Bestsellers Look Behind You, Untouchable, Duplicity, and Into the Darkness. Her books have sold over one million copies and are international bestsellers in the UK, USA, Australia, France, Canada and Germany. She writes in an eclectic mix of genres, and is a passionate human and animal rights advocate.

Her work has been nominated and shortlisted for numerous prizes, including the Harry Bowling Prize, the Yeovil Literary Prize, the Chapter One Promotions Novel Competition, The Romance Reviews' prize for Best Novel with Romantic Elements and Indie Book Bargains' Best Indie Book of 2012 in two categories. She was the winner of Best Children's Book in the 2013 eFestival of Words; nominated for the 2015 BigAl's Books and Pals Young Adult Readers' Choice Award; winner of the Crime, Thrillers & Mystery Book from a Series Award in the SpaSpa Book Awards 2013; winner of the Readers' Favorite Young Adult (Coming of Age) Honorable award in 2015; a New Adult finalist in the Oklahoma Romance Writers of America's International Digital Awards 2015, 2017 International Thriller Writers Award finalist for Best E-book Original Novel, Honorable Mention Award Winner in the USA 2018 Reader's Choice Awards, and winner of the No 1 Best Thriller in the Top Shelf Magazine Indie Book Awards 2018! Her novella Trafficked: The Diary of a Sex Slave has been listed as one of the top forty books about human rights by Accredited Online Colleges.

For Sibel's latest book releases, giveaways and gossip, sign up to her newsletter at: www.sibelhodge.com

Also by Sibel Hodge

Non-Fiction

Healing Meditations for Surviving Grief and Loss

Fiction

The Disappeared
Into the Darkness
Beneath the Surface
Duplicity
Untouchable
Where the Memories Lie
Look Behind You
Butterfly
Trafficked: The Diary of a Sex Slave
Fashion, Lies, and Murder (Amber Fox Mystery No 1)
Money, Lies, and Murder (Amber Fox Mystery No 2)
Voodoo, Lies, and Murder (Amber Fox Mystery No 3)
Chocolate, Lies, and Murder (Amber Fox Mystery No 4)
Santa Claus, Lies, and Murder (Amber Fox Mystery No 4.5)
Vegas, Lies, and Murder (Amber Fox Mystery No 5)
Murder and Mai Tais (Danger Cove Cocktail Mystery No 1)
Killer Colada (Danger Cove Cocktail Mystery No 2)
The See-Through Leopard
Fourteen Days Later
My Perfect Wedding
The Baby Trap
It's a Catastrophe

Printed in Great Britain
by Amazon